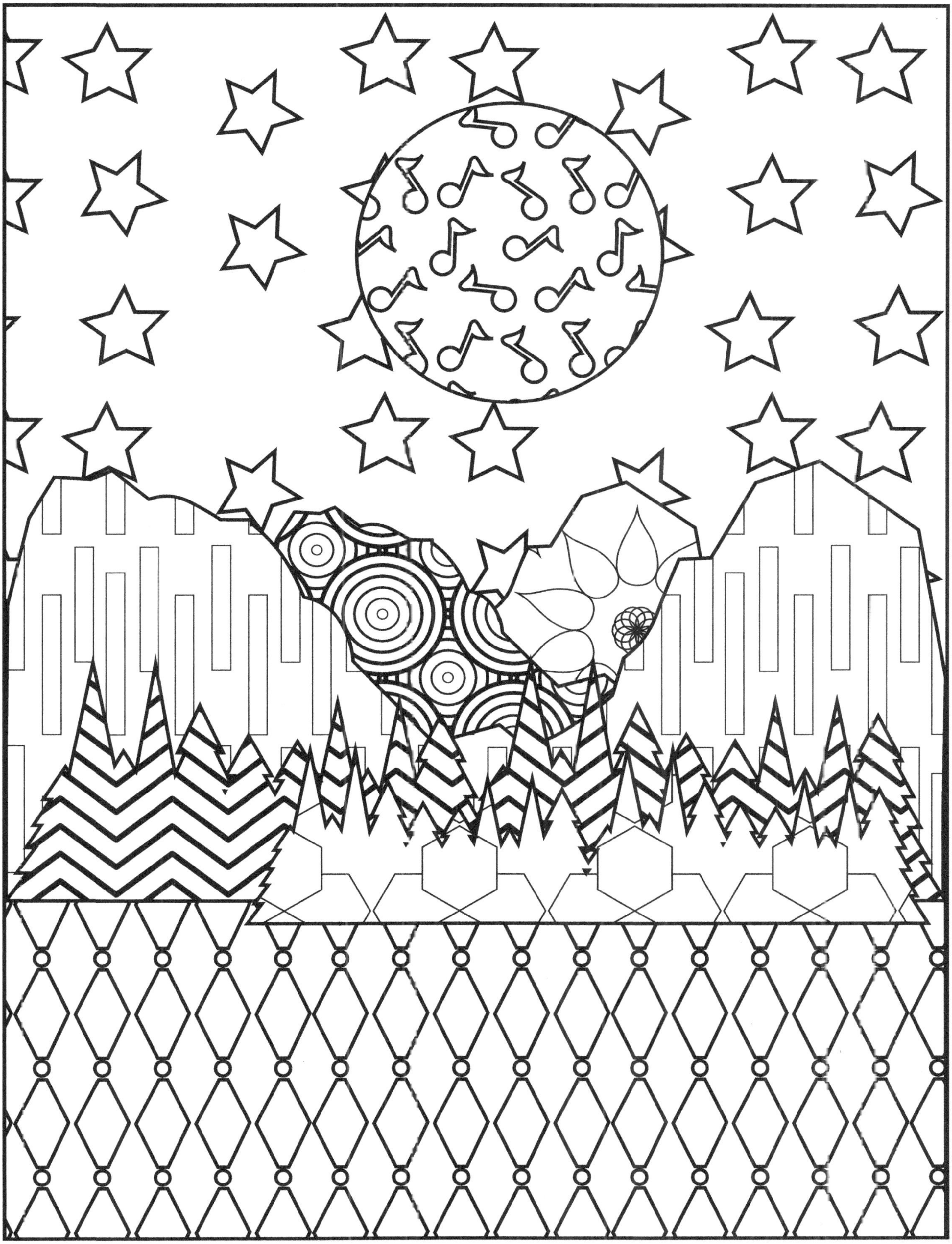

FRESNO

FRESNO

Raisins

Raisins

Tower
Tower

Tower
Tower

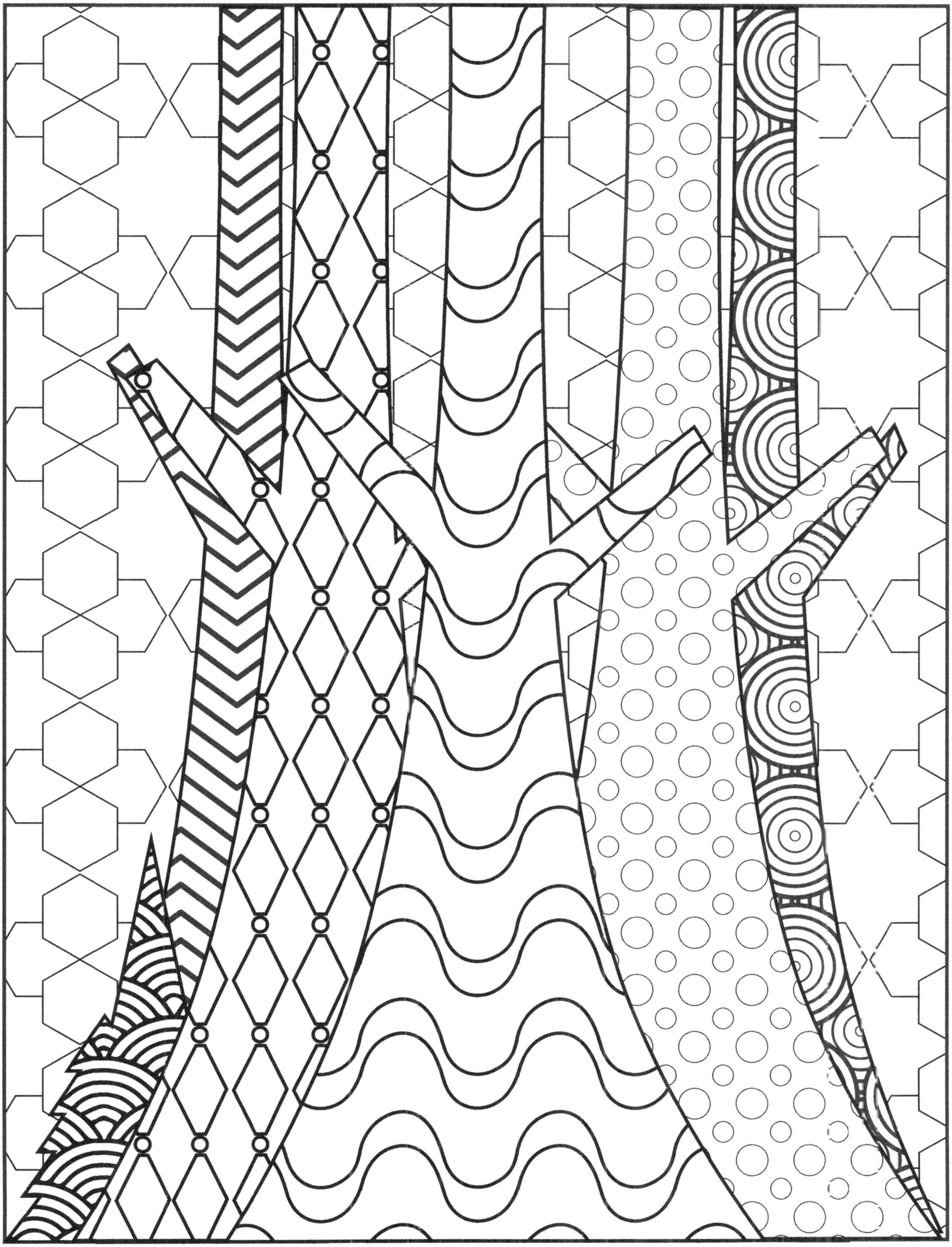

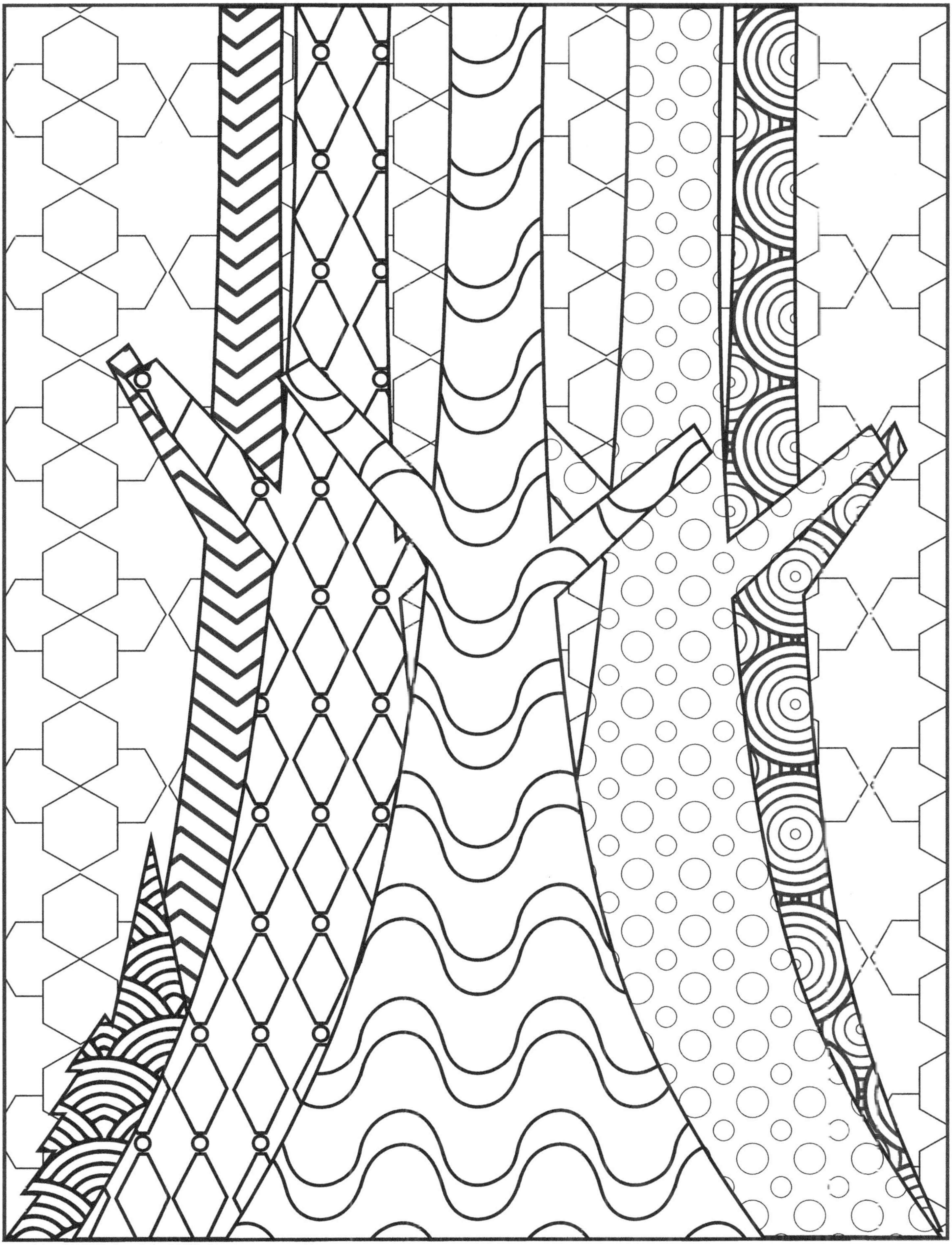

FRESNO

FRESNO

Raisins

Raisins

FRESNO

FRESNO

Tower

SF

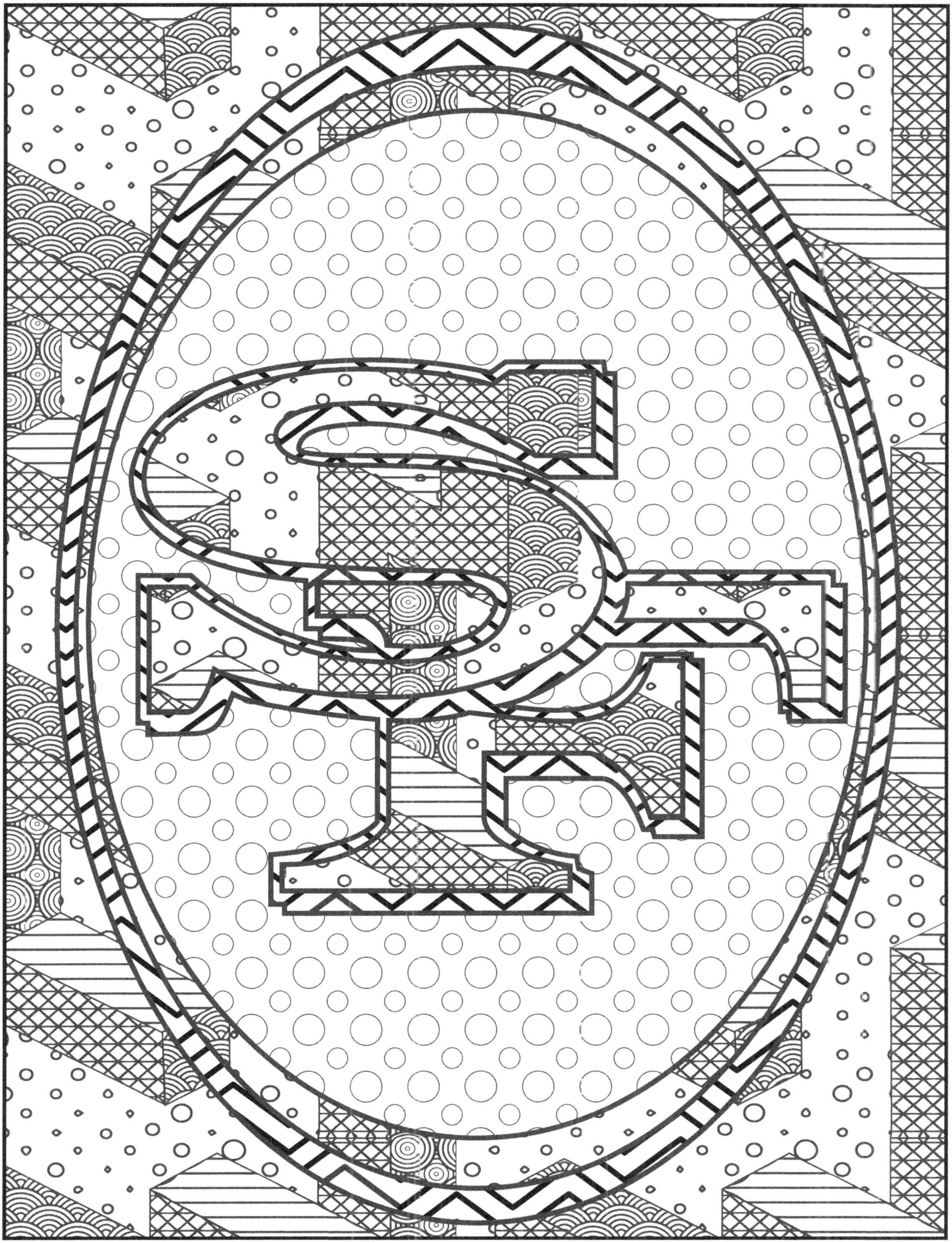
SF

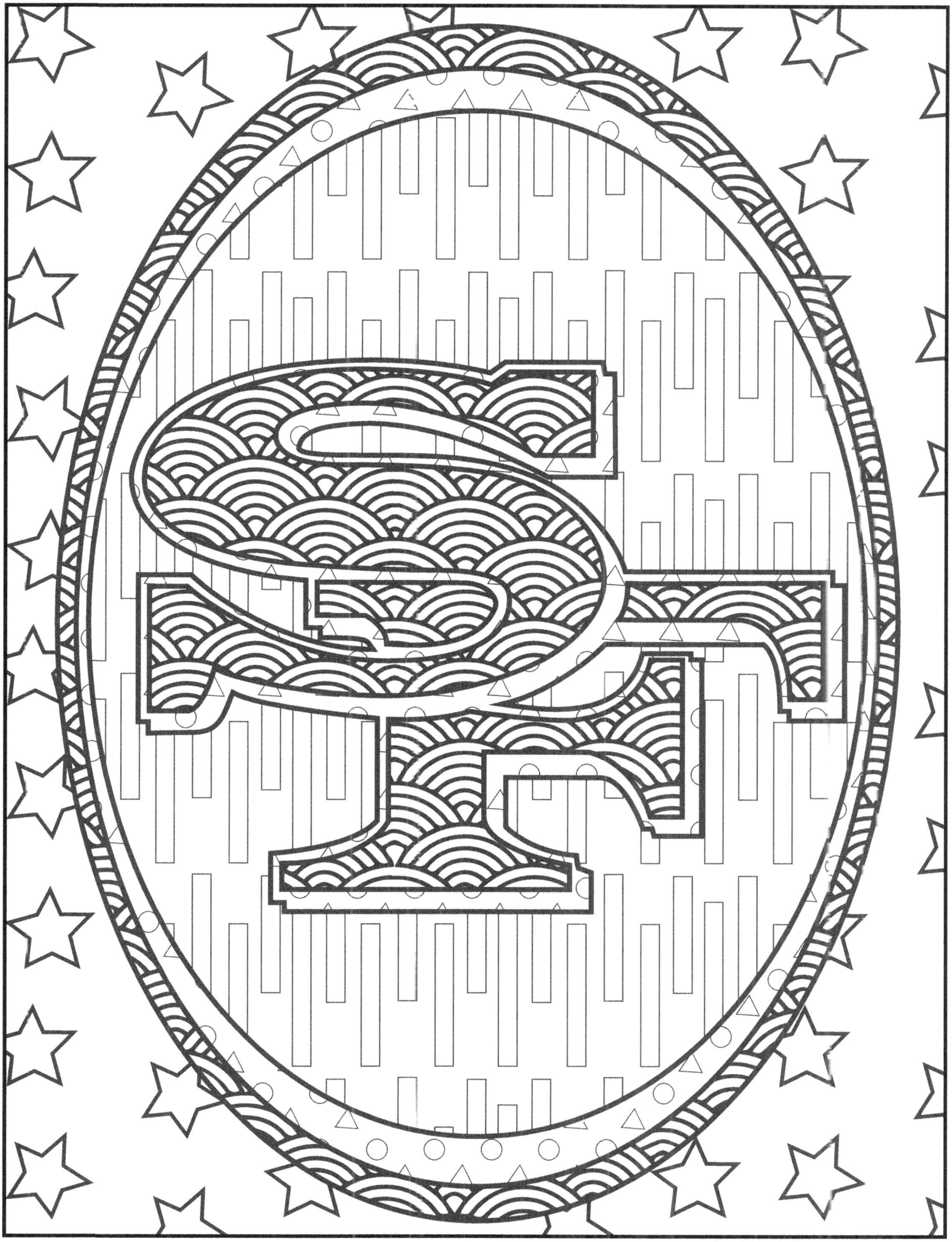

SF

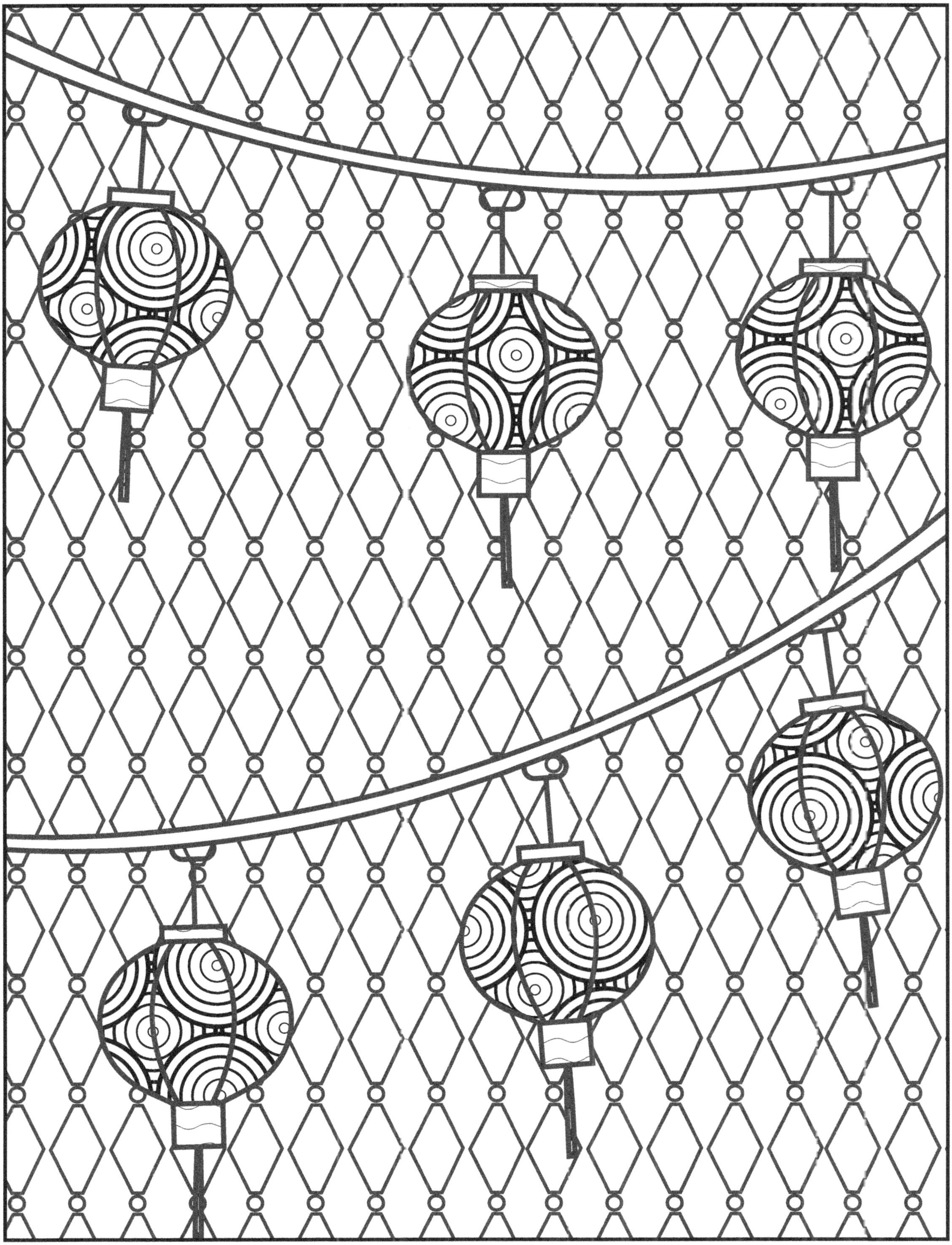

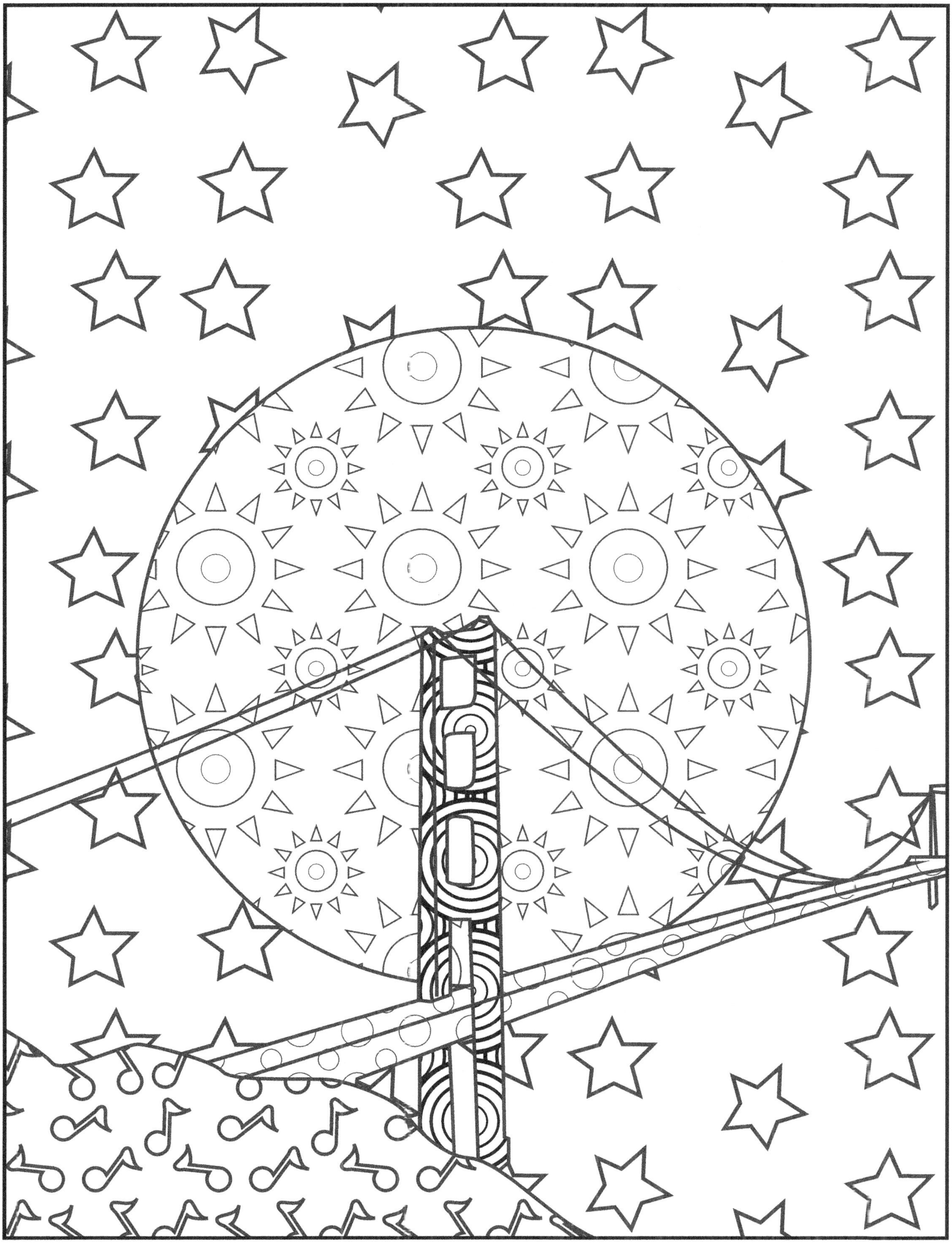

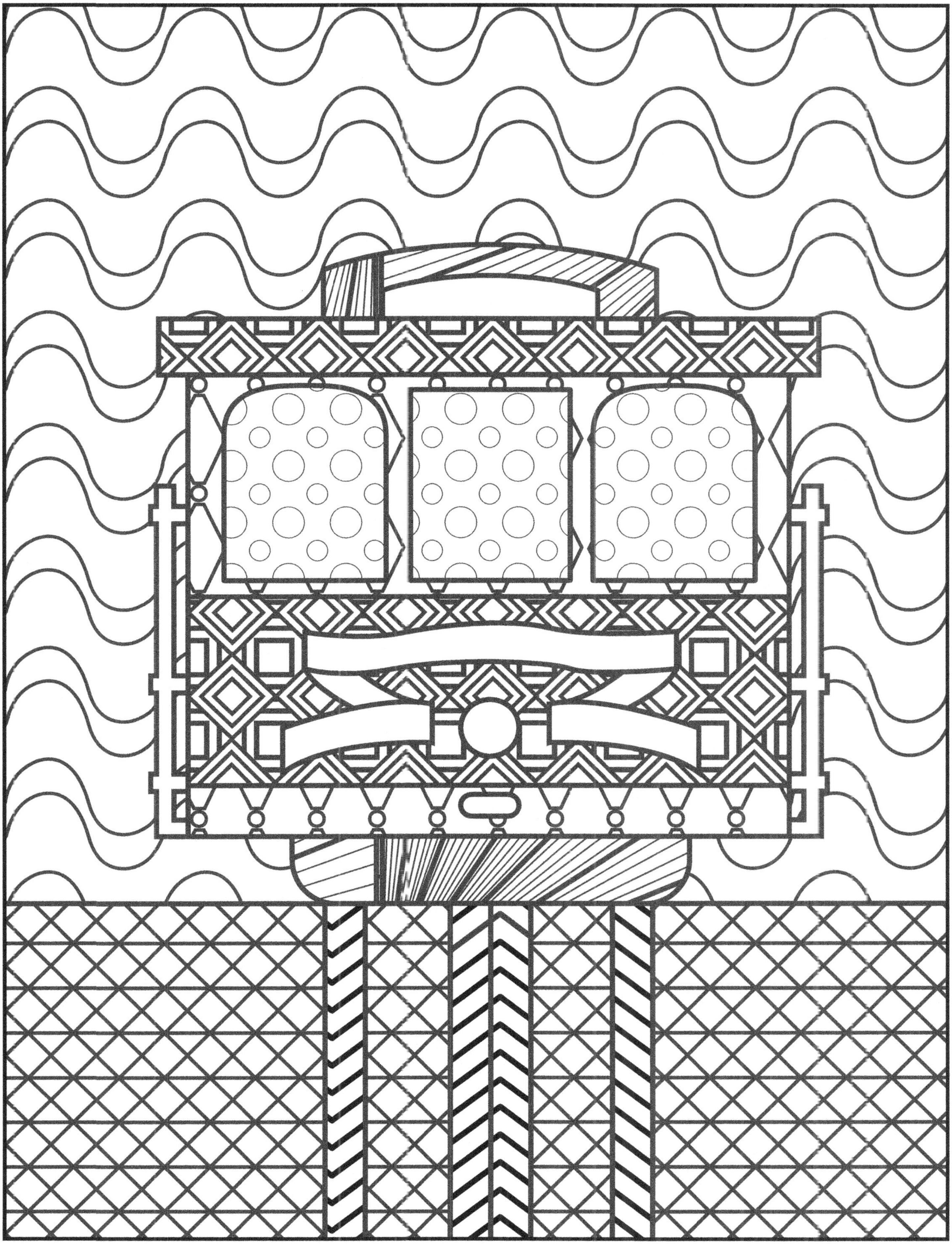

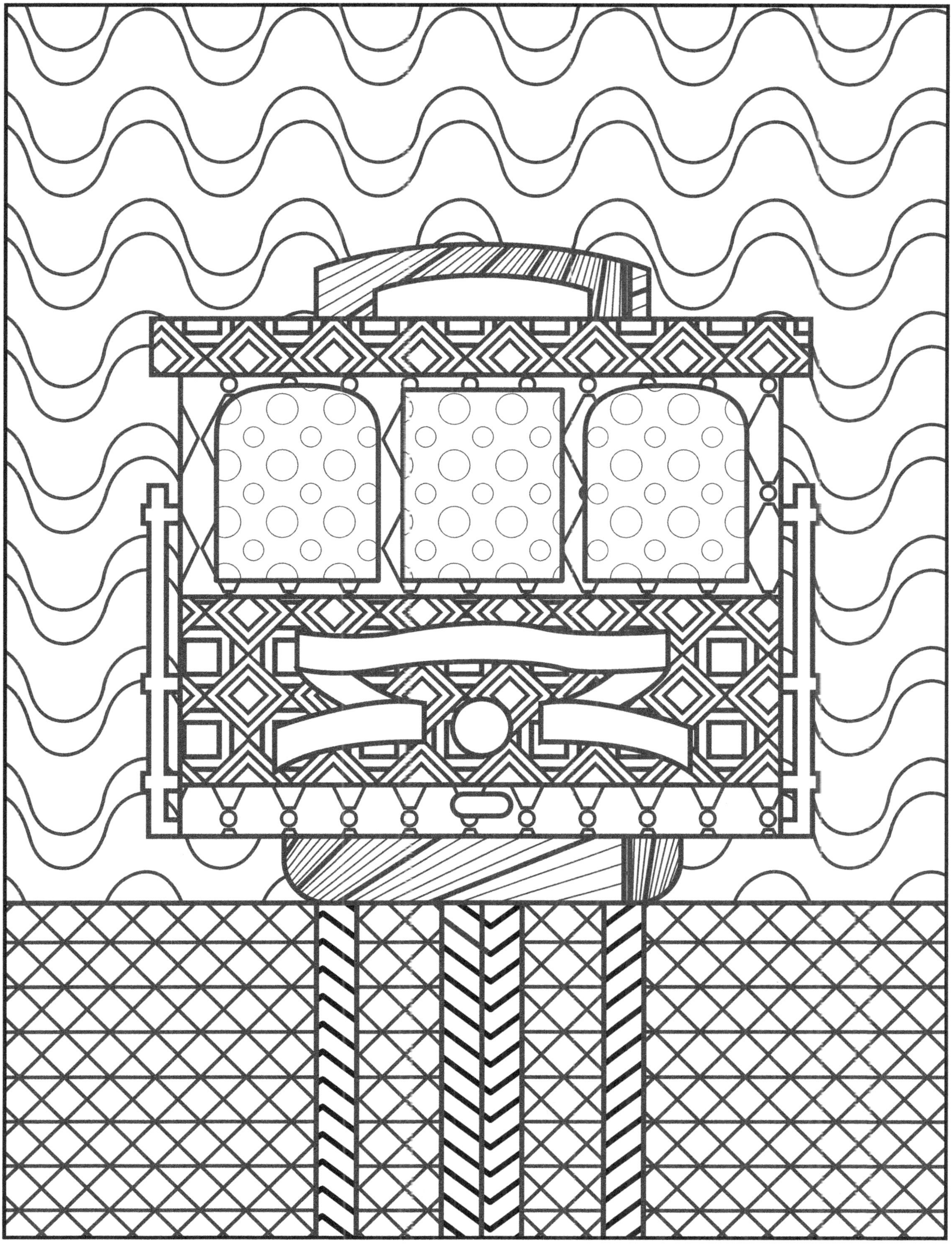

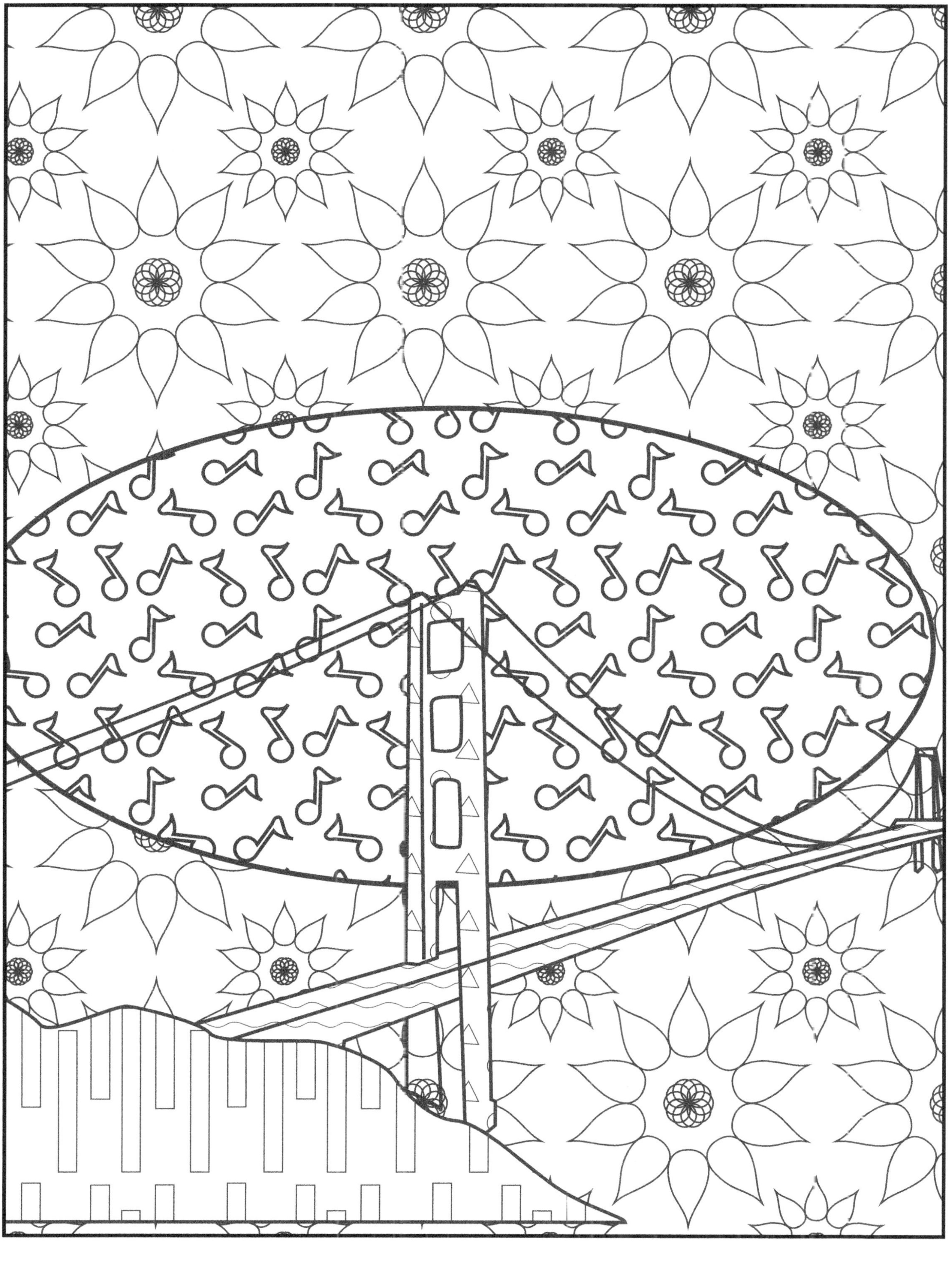

Made in the USA
Monee, IL
15 February 2021

60534544R00070